Perspectives

The Big, Bad Wolf
True or False?

T0359782

Series Consultant: Linda Hoyt

Flying Start
to Literacy®

Contents

Introduction

Why should the wolf always be "big and bad?"

Do you know the story of "Little Red Riding Hood" or "The Three Little Pigs"?

There are many children's stories, songs and games that involve wolves, and most times, the wolf is a fierce, scary character!

Why is the wolf shown in this way? Where did the idea of the "big, bad wolf" begin?

Wolves: Why do we think they're bad?

Written by Kerrie Shanahan

From a very young age, we have heard stories about big, bad wolves: wolves that blow down houses, scare little children and eat grandmothers.

Why is the wolf always the "bad guy"?

Why do we believe this?

Wolves were first described as dangerous and frightening long ago, when people began to settle in wilderness areas. These settlers cleared the land to set up farms, and the wolves living in those areas lost their home territory.

Because the wolves had less land to roam in and less prey to feed on, they sometimes attacked the farmers' livestock. And this is where it all began – they became the enemy.

The wolf is a smart animal that uses very clever hunting techniques to catch its prey. Because of this, people saw the wolf as being cunning. This grew into describing the storybook wolf as a sly and dishonest character that shouldn't be trusted.

At first, wolf stories were told as a way of warning young children of the dangers of wandering into the woods alone. These stories were added to and passed on from generation to generation . . . and still we hear them today.

Speak out!

Are all wolves big and bad?

Read what these students have to say.

Wolves are wild because they live in the forest. They are carnivores. So if you go into their habitat, then you could be in trouble. You could be attacked. If you think they are violent for no good reason, think again – we have gone into their space.

Not all wolves are the same. Wolves are called big and bad because wolves steal people's animals. Wolves need to eat too.

Have you ever thought why the big, bad wolf is called the "big, bad wolf"? Why don't we call a lion the "big, bad lion"? I think it's because of stories like "Little Red Riding Hood" and "The Three Little Pigs". The real question is, are wolves really bad?

The house dog and the wolf

Written by Robin Cruise

Some dogs look very much like wolves. In what ways do you think they are the same or different?

One day, a wolf wandered out of the forest and met a house dog.

"Brother, you look just like me," said the wolf. "But I am skinny and you are fat."

"You can be fat, too," said the house dog. "I have a master that feeds me. He will feed you, too."

"Really?" said the wolf. "Take me to him."

As the wolf and the house dog walked towards the dog's house, the wolf noticed a red band around the dog's neck.

"What is that around your neck?" asked the wolf.

"It's my collar," said the house dog.

"What's it for?" asked the wolf.

"So my master can tie me up to stop me from wandering away," said the house dog.

"Do you mean you cannot go wherever you like whenever you want?" asked the wolf.

"That's not important to me," said the dog, "because my master feeds me very well."

"My freedom is important to me," said the wolf, and he turned and ran back into the forest.

A tale of two wolves

This story comes from a group of Native American people called Cherokee. It has been passed down for many generations. What message is the grandfather telling the boy?

A man told his grandson:

"My child, there is a battle between two wolves
inside us all.

One is bad. It is anger, jealousy and greed.
It tells lies and feels resentful.

The other is good. It is joy, peace and love.
It tells the truth and is hopeful and kind."

The boy thought about it, and asked:

"Grandfather, which wolf wins?"

The old man quietly replied:

"The one you choose to feed."

How to write about your opinion

State your opinion

Think about the main question in the introduction on page 4 of this book. What is your opinion?

Research

Look for other information that you need to back up your opinion.

Related information book
Saving Wild Wolves

Internet

Other sources

Make a plan

Introduction

How will you "hook" the reader to get them interested?

Write a sentence that makes your opinion clear.

List reasons to support your opinion.

Support your reason with examples.

Support your reason with examples.

Support your reason with examples.

Conclusion

Write a sentence that makes your opinion clear. Leave your reader with a strong message.

Publish

Publish your writing.

Include some graphics or visual images.

© 2020 EC Licensing Pty. Ltd.